I AM A BLACK
WOMAN

Mari Evans

I AM A BLACK WOMAN

William Morrow and Company, Inc.

1970

NEW YORK

The title poem, *I Am A Black Woman,* appeared originally in *Negro Digest (Black World).* Other poems appeared originally in the following magazines and anthologies: *American Negro Poetry,* edited by Arna Bontemps, Hill & Wang; *Arts in Society; Black Voices,* edited by Abraham Chapman, New American Library; *Freedomways; For Malcolm,* edited by Margaret Burroughs and Dudley Randall, Broadside Press; *Negro Digest (Black World); New Negro Poets: USA,* edited by Langston Hughes, Indiana University Press; *Poets of Today,* edited by Walter Lowenfels, International Publishers.

Photograph on page 14 by Al Fenner.

Photographs on pages 28, 40, 52, and 64 by Bob Fletcher.

Photograph on title page and page 94 by Thomas Jackson.

Printed in the United States of America.

Library of Congress Catalog Card Number 72-121690

For Evan, Derek, and The Root

CONTENTS

I AM A BLACK
WOMAN

I Am A Black Woman

I am a black woman
the music of my song
some sweet arpeggio of tears
is written in a minor key
and I
can be heard humming in the night
Can be heard
                    humming
in the night

I saw my mate leap screaming to the sea
and I/with these hands/cupped the lifebreath
from my issue in the canebrake
I lost Nat's swinging body in a rain of tears
and heard my son scream all the way from Anzio
for Peace he never knew. . . . I
learned Da Nang and Pork Chop Hill
in anguish
Now my nostrils know the gas
and these trigger tire/d fingers
seek the softness in my warrior's beard

I
am a black woman
tall as a cypress
strong
beyond all definition still
defying place
and time
and circumstance
  assailed
    impervious
      indestructible
Look
  on me and be
renewed

I AM A BLACK
WOMAN

"TO THESE ADD ONE:
LOVE WITHHELD
RESTRAINED"

If There Be Sorrow

If there be sorrow
let it be
for things undone
undreamed
    unrealized
       unattained

to these add one:
love withheld
   restrained

I Who Would Encompass Millions

I
who would encompass
millions
am adrift on
this
my single
bed

The Silver Cell

I have
never been contained
except I
made
the prison, nor
known a chain
except those forged
by me

O I am slave
and I am master
am at once
both bound
and
free

Conflict

I know with pain
the Me that
is, and I
inbreathe
this anguish deep
upon my heart

I
keen and flail
behind my
tight-squeezed lids
much too aware
to stay

and
seemingly unable
to depart

To Mother and Steve

All I wanted
was your
love

when I roiled down
Brewster blew
soft pot clouds on
subs when
I lay in nameless rooms
cold-sweating
horse in nameless arms
crawled
thru white hell owning
no one no one no one save
one purple-bruised soul
pawned
in exchange for
oblivion
   all I wanted
was
your love

not twice but
constantly
I tried
to free you

it was all
such cold shit
then
the last day
of the
last year
of my raw-edged anguish
I was able wearily
at last—
to roll.

(all I wanted
was
your love)
I bought this final
battered gift

(do not refuse—for it
was all
I had)

with my back supported
by the tolerant
arms
of a picket fence and my
legs crumpled crazily in front
and love fell
soft and cold and
covered me in
blanket
like

the one you
tucked around me
centuries
ago and like that
later
gently pulled
across my face
and in this season
of peace and
goodwill and the smell
of cedar
remembered
thru warm yellow
windows—
    all I wanted
and it was more than
I could stand and
more than a thousand passions and
I could not
mainline it
away

        was your
        love

I Can No Longer Sing

I can no longer
sing

the fluid beauty
which once fled my soul
to hang quicksilvered
in the mote-filled
air
has gone, stripped
is my heart
joy lies discarded
near and I
am naked
in my silence

Thin-Sliced

warm me with your fingertips
your breath your
lips
        I
understand your
heart
belongs to each new
smile
     and what small love
     you have must
be retained
for your own
chill

Here—Hold My Hand

Here
hold my hand
let me touch you
there is
nothing
we can
say ... your
soul
eludes me
when I reach
out
your eyes
resent
my need to know
you

here
hold my hand
since
there is nothing
we can
say

into blackness softly

the hesitant door chain
back forth back
forth
    the
stealthy
    soft
       final
          sssshuuu t
jubilantly
    stepping down
      stepping down
        step
ping lightly across the lower
    hall
the shocking airfingers
    the
      receiving

       blackness

  sigh

I AM A BLACK
WOMAN

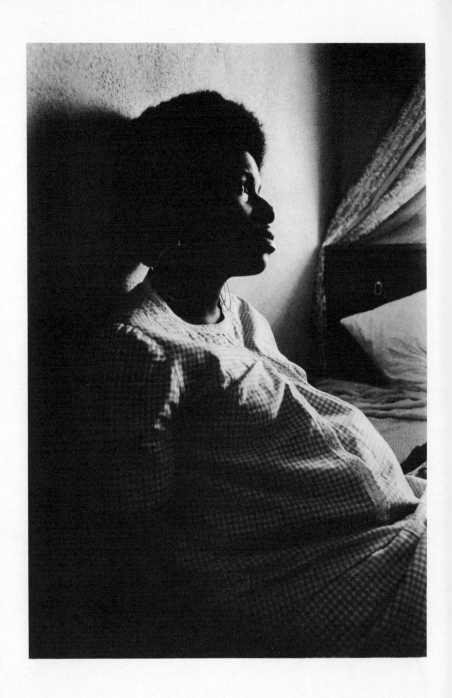

"...MY VACANT HEART
ROCKS GENTLY
IN THE WAKE OF
MY DEPARTED"

In the Wake of My Departed

I have tasted alien
mouths and felt the sinews
of an arm
not worn like yours with
one place
that my head had learned

The hot and foreign
brinedrops
insistent whispers
all
a litany repeated while
you mock me from the shadows
while my tightened eyes
pierce shadows

and my vacant heart
rocks gently
in the wake of my departed

hegira

I
was not here
when you called
last night
            I
was a mist in Taipei
a crimson glow
that passed for neon
on Broadway
a soft haze
in an Avenue tavern

It was you
I
sought

Marrow of My Bone

Fondle me
caress
and cradle
me
with your lips
withdraw
the nectar from
me
teach me there
is
someone

I Am Not Lazy

Living
is
too much
effort ...
I
am not
lazy
just
battered ...
I
cannot make
the
valiant push
the
all-for-God-and
country
the good-old-college
try

one
bullet ... now

this
coup de grâce is
such a small thing

and so
kind

I am not
lazy ... just
... battered

Where Have You Gone

Where have you gone

with your confident
walk with
your crooked smile

why did you leave
me
when you took your
laughter
and departed

are you aware that
with you
went the sun
all light
and what few stars
there were?

where have you gone
with your confident
walk your
crooked smile the
rent money
in one pocket and
my heart
in another ...

... if i had a gun that would shoot

if i had a gun that would shoot
i would put one bullet
through my wearied
brain
relieve my soul
of its
responsibility
to
weep ...
release my
heart
from its unrelievedness
my hands
my hands
of their wilting inadequacy
my mind
of its
desperate circling
if i had a gun
that would
shoot ...

And the hotel room
held only him

And the hotel room held only
him

    and the alarm would ring
    and he would dress
    and lock the door

and the hotel room held only
him

    and the bus would come
    and he would open his paper
    and then he would nod

and the hotel room held only
him

    and the hot dank coffee smelled of people
    and fans whirred, drawers slammed, typewriters
        clattered
    and emptied eyes excluded him

and the hotel room held only
him

    and he just missed the last seat on the bus
    and he sat a long time in the cafeteria over his paper
    and he walked slowly down the neoned streets

and the hotel room held only
him

    and he threw up his hand and smiled at the desk clerk
    and he took the half-silent self-service to seven
    and he walked slowly down the worn corridor

    and he unlocked his door and closed it ... slowly

and the hotel room held only
him

I AM A BLACK
WOMAN

"LET ME CROOK MY ARM
AROUND THEM
THE MILLIONS . . .
THE CHILDBODIES"

escape

theodore R. the III
finally
got past aunt clelia uncle
dan and the
heavy glassed front
door which
protected
him from the
Other Kids
and ran ran ran ran ran ran ran
ran ran ran ran ran
ran ran ran ran
ran ran ran ran ran
it
took seven
Other Kids
to catch him:
gently—for
they greatly admired
his defiance . . .
aunt clelia only stood there
damp handed
on the
empty front
porch

To a Child That Was

I never knew your loneliness
and knowing now
I die
for soul so lost so
desolate for anguished
eyes
and dry for spirit
bruised for love
not given, knowledge
thus realized
is bitter hemlock
brew well earned a
proper legacy
from you ...
for loneliness
is also death
and sorrow
must be
learned

Uhuru Überalles!
(. . . and the sound
of weeping)

solemnly
they gathered in
oakpaneled offices
overlooking the Hudson
the Trinity
the Moskva the
Yungting ..
ceiling to floor anguish
wall-to-wall blood
amidst all this
beauty they spoke
ruefully
      "Save
            the world ..."
and they dried their tears
with money

and the green
streaked their faces
their
whitefaces
brownblackyellow faces and
cries

of Libertad!
   Ungebundenheit!
      Liberty!
in brown/black/yellow/andred
filled the air

and those without shoes
heard and echoed
and the noise of their
patriotism
brought tears which they
wiped
with the backs of their
      h a n d s
their whitehands
brownblackyellowredhands
and they gathered their
young
   beautiful
      valiant
their white brownblackyellowred shafts
      of flame and tenderness
         and taught them the
               art
         of ... dying.

And the Fathers
the oilsteeltextilesmunitions
graincattlesugar
ore Fathers
          white
brownyellowblackred Fathers
in oakpaneled offices overlooking every
                    scenic port on
                    Earth

cried softly Liberty!
          Libertad!
          Ungebundenheit!
and wiped their tears
                    with/
                         money

Apologia

Let me crook my arm around them
the millions ...
the saffronbrown childbodies
pulsating
warm slight heartbeats
adorable
round starvation
bellies
yet these few fleet
seconds
let me
crook my arm around them
offering compassion for
like you

I send not bread but
napalm
IN THE NAME OF PEACE
AND THE TRIUNE
GOD

Grits and Rice Grains

this
savory mouthful
mine

I
feed on
tears
and leave my plate
untouched
except by

guilt

The Friday Ladies of the Pay Envelope

they take
stations
in the broken doorways
the narrow alcoves
and the flaking
gray paint
the rainandsoot paint
clings
to their limpworn
sweaters clings
hair and limpworn souls they
wait
for the sullen
triumph
for the crumpled lifeblood
wet with reluctance
thrust
        at them
in the direction
of them
     of their reaching
of their drydamp
  limpworn hands

Rout

treading air
    eyes wide against the
        horror

you delicately maneuver

through
the rubbish jungle steer
      a
broken field through
heedless cars
practised and resolutely

fleeing
an infinite and private
hell

I AM A BLACK
WOMAN

"I'M GOING TO RISE
EN MASSE
FROM
INNER CITY"

The Emancipation of
George-Hector
(a colored turtle)

George-Hector
is
spoiled.
formerly he stayed
well up in his
shell ... but now
he hangs arms and legs
sprawlingly
in a most langorous fashion
head rared back
to
be
admired

he didn't use to
talk ...
but
he does now.

The 7:25 Trolley

ain't got time for a bite to eat
I'll have to run to catch my trolley at the end of the block
and if I take
my coffee
there
she looks at the cup and she looks at the clock
            (Sure hope I don't miss my car . . .

my house looks like a hurricane
if I did what I ought to do I'd stay at home today
I can't eat no
hurricane
broke as I am I need what she will pay
            (Hope I just don't miss my car . . .

wish my life was a life of ease
a maid cook and butler runnin' at my beck and call
I may scrub floors
but
I don't
get on my knees . . .
and someday
I won't go at all
            (Sure hope I don't miss my car . . .

When in Rome

Mattie dear
the box is full
take
whatever you like
to eat
        (an egg
        or soup
        ... there ain't no meat)

there's endive there
and
cottage cheese
        (whew! if I had some
        black-eyed peas ...)

there's sardines
on the shelves
and such
but
don't
get my anchovies

they cost
too much!
        (me get the
        anchovies indeed!
        what she think, she got—
        a bird to feed?)

there's plenty in there
to fill you up.
            (yes'm. just the
            sight's
            enough!

            Hope I lives till I get
            home
            I'm tired of eatin'
            what they eats in Rome ...)

beATrice does the dinner

beATrice has the dinner done
mmmmm just smell that food
"Bee—what are you cookin' hon
shure enough smells good!

tuna fish en casserole
salad, rolls and tea!

      (Gread Day In The Mornin'
          s t i l l
        no blackeyed peas!)

The Alarm Clock

Alarm clock
sure sound
loud
this mornin'

remind me of the time
I sat down
in a drug store
with my mind
a way far off

until the girl
and she was small
it seems to me
with yellow hair
a hangin'
smiled up and said
'I'm sorry but
we don't serve
you people
here'
and I woke up
quick
like I did this mornin'
when the

alarm
went off

It don't do
to wake up
quick

early in the mornin

early in the mornin
j w brown
whippin' his woman
knockin' her around
said "answer my question
if you please"
(how she goin' to answer
on her knees
groanin' 'Buddy, Buddy!
wake up and go
get L C and Mar'gret—he's
hurtin' me so . .')

Buddy went flyin'
down the stairs in
brown pants over his
underwear but
L C and Margaret wouldn't stir
said: "Buddy we sympathize
with her . . . but from what you say
far as we can see
if she'd answer his question
he'd let her be"

she never did answer
(far as we could hear)

but the sight of that child
in his underwear his
head bent down
shoes untied and all
comin' back alone
down the empty Mall
was sad.
More than I could bear.
Makes you wonder if
anybody cares
anywhere

I AM A BLACK
WOMAN

"A BLACK ONENESS, A BLACK STRENGTH"

The Great Civil Rights Law (A. D. 1964)

        they called
Grateful meetings
        did
Grateful dances
        to the pulse of
Grateful drums

while the Faces smiled
with knowing that the
        Beads
which made   /them/
Grateful
had been formed from trees felled by Black hands
shaped in grief by Black tears
dipped for centuries in Black blood
belonged
in fact
to a Black God Almighty Himself

                i/
will not sit
in Grateful meetings

                    i/
cannot do
the Grateful dances
cannot hear
the Grateful drums

the Beads were   /mine/
before you stole them

given
as I
stepped
from
out the womb ...

status symbol

i
Have Arrived

i
am the
New Negro

i
am the result of
President Lincoln
World War I
and Paris
the
Red Ball Express
white drinking fountains
sitdowns and
sit-ins
Federal Troops
Marches on Washington
and
prayer meetings
today
They hired me

it
is a status
job ...

along
with my papers
They
gave me my
Status Symbol

the
key
to the
White ... Locked ...
John

Vive Noir!

i
am going to rise
en masse
from Inner City

                  sick
               of newyork ghettos
               chicago tenements
          l   a's slums
weary
      of exhausted lands
      sagging privies
      saying yessuh yessah
      yesSIR
      in an assortment
      of geographical dialects i
have seen my last
broken down plantation
even from a
distance
       i
will load all my goods
in '50 Chevy pickups '53
Fords fly United and '66
caddys i
      have packed in
      the old man and the old lady and

              wiped the children's noses
                        I'm tired
                            of hand me downs
                                shut me ups
                                    pin me ins
                                        keep me outs
                                            messing me over have
                                        just had it
                            baby
                    from
              you ...
i'm
gonna spread out
over America
            intrude
my proud blackness
all
        over the place
                        i have wrested wheat fields
                        from the forests

                        turned rivers
                        from their courses

                        leveled mountains
                        at a word
                        festooned the land with
                        bridges
                                    gemlike
                            on filaments of steel
                                    moved

          glistening towersofBabel in place
                    like blocks
          sweated a whole
          civilization

               now
                         i'm
          gonna breathe fire
          through flaming nostrils BURN
                    a place for

                    me

          in the skyscrapers and the
          schoolrooms on the green
          lawns and the white
          beaches
                         i'm
          gonna wear the robes and
          sit on the benches
          make the rules and make
          the arrests say
          who can and who
          can't

                         baby you don't stand
                         a
                         chance
     i'm
          gonna put black angels
          in all the books and a black
          Christchild in Mary's arms i'm
          gonna make black bunnies black

fairies black santas black
nursery rhymes and
                    black
ice cream
                i'm
gonna make it a
    crime
            to be anything BUT   black
            pass the coppertone

gonna make white
a twentyfourhour
lifetime
J.O.B.
        an' when all the coppertone's gone. . .?

things IS changing

bus driver say
  MOVE BACK!

        he use
    th' wrong
voice

say
    sixty dollars chi/ange own
    wun run!!! aint thay'ut
    ridiculous!
Willetta say
whuts
th'madduhwidyou?
dont they give you
no change?
Mattie Bell
say
I got sumthin' in here
make him dance $^{up}_{an'}$ down

Folks dont
takenoshit   nowadays

        Ev'abodys evil.

The Insurgent

I take my freedom
lest I die
for pride runs through my veins
not blood
and principles
support me so that
I
with lifted head see
Liberty
        not sky!
For I am he who
dares to say
I shall be Free, or dead
today ...

The Rebel

When I
die
I'm sure
I will have a
Big Funeral

Curiosity
seekers

coming to see
if I
am really
Dead

or just
trying to make
Trouble

Black jam for dr. negro

Pullin me in off the corner to wash my face an
cut my fro off turn
my collar
down
when that aint my
thang I
walk heels first
nose round an tilted
up
my ancient
eyes
see your thang
baby
an it aint
shit
your thang
puts my eyes out baby
turns my seeking fingers
    into splintering fists
messes up my head
an I scream you out
your thang
is what's   wrong
    an' you keep
    pilin it on rubbin it

in
smoothly
doin it
to death

what you sweatin
baby
                   your guts
puked an rotten
waitin'

to be defended

Flames

There is no beauty
to the world I see
save moments stopped in
time
preserved
in unreality

blood from the streets
from the dim bayou
surges
and the river of it
clouds
my view till hate
with a wild candescent blue
purges
what was love
burns me
free
of you

there are no birds
no sky
no sea and
only hate
stares back
at me

where
is the music
I would feel

I hear no song

. . . just my hate
is real

princeling

swing sweet rhythm
     charcoal toes
swing sweet rhythm
        blooddripped knees
swing sweet rhythm
       exorcised penis
swing sweet rhythm
        My God—my son!

My Man Let Me Pull Your Coat . . .

All praise be to
Allah
only the
mistakes . . .
are mine
       the otherness
       the cries
       the implorations
       all
       the blue smoke
       the acrid stink
       the white bodies
       the cold cell
       and the outstretched hands
          unbelieving
          opening
          learning
          grasping
          sharing
          pounding
          tearing
          splintering
          shrieking upraised proud

cacophony of hate   love
salvation
to lie smeared
blood-red over the hearts
and cobblestones
of a nation shamed
slinking silently from the
          love beats
expiring softly
before the brethren
Labbayka!
          My Man—let me . . .

A good assassination should be quiet

he had
A Dream
e x p loded
down
his
th r o a t.

whereon
a million hard white eyes
swung impiously heavenward
to mourn
the gross indelicate demise

Such public death
transgresses
all known rules

A good assassination
should be quiet

and occupy the heart
four hundred
years

eyes gentled at the corners so

How many death songs will we write?

Can we eulogize
sufficiently
the torn
the bleeding
   all
The Dead
        dead flesh
        dead hopes
        dead smiles

Can we count the wasted
hours fill the days to come with
flaking blood/ instead of Men?

Neither chants nor wails nor mournings fill
the emptied place obscure the memory nor
heal the heart, what
compensates for
eyes ...
        gentled at the corners so
   from loving

The Young BlackandBeautiful in Pursuit of Ancient Freedomdreams

They adorn themselves lovingly
   and go forth
their sandaled feet will lie
  later
    in the gutterdust
       their blood will mat
       their leopard robes and
       from the gutterdust
      their proud black beards
     will point accusingly
      at Heaven

Uhuru

Fingers
flaming interclenched
blood to blood
The cold breath of our laughter
but a single wind
Your eye warm to mine shared
presentpast and ancient source
Black unison
our heartbeats

Remembered Rhythms

(The Individuals)

Insistent rhythms
  feeding black fingers
  moving black heads
  tilting black shoulders

  bending
  resilient innovative
  owning all patterns

Remembered rhythms
sinuous
black
  powering to Oneness

(The Group)

Brothers concealed in the blue midnight cavern lights
held by erudite and funky phrases shaped from
twisted notes powered by new rhythms
fierce rhythms insistent
remembered from some ancientsource
Brothers
instructing each other in beauty
survival
Love

Whisper Together
Brethren

Whisper together brethren
Glide thru the darkness
Thru the darkness black
        like you
Thru ancestral blackness
Glide alone, in pairs
Thru ancestral blackness where one match
Burns brighter than a thousand slogans and one
        bullet speaks
Louder than a million marching feet
For every Black Man's murdered back
Death is the equalizer
        There is a company with us
        That should have ceased to be ...
Whisper together brethren
Glide through the darkness

Brother . . . the twilight

brother . . .
The twilight of your loins
an eerie white encroaching
on your black fire
coldcircling all your beauty
your black strength
Mingle your warm love with mine
and with our last hands fling
the sweet black shit of our resistance
at the whitefaced
ovens . . .

Speak the Truth to the People

Speak the truth to the people
Talk sense to the people
Free them with reason
Free them with honesty
Free the people with Love and Courage and Care for
       their Being
Spare them the fantasy
Fantasy enslaves
A slave is enslaved
Can be enslaved by unwisdom
Can be enslaved by black unwisdom
Can be re-enslaved while in flight from the enemy
Can be enslaved by his brother whom he loves
His brother whom he trusts
His brother with the loud voice
And the unwisdom
Speak the truth to the people
It is not necessary to green the heart
Only to identify the enemy
It is not necessary to blow the mind
Only to free the mind
To identify the enemy is to free the mind
A free mind has no need to scream
A free mind is ready for other things

To BUILD black schools
To BUILD black children
To BUILD black minds
To BUILD black love
To BUILD black impregnability
To BUILD a strong black nation
To BUILD.

Speak the truth to the people.
Spare them the opium of devil-hate.
They need no trips on honky-chants.
Move them instead to a BLACK ONENESS.
A black strength which will defend its own
Needing no cacophony of screams for activation
A black strength which attacks the laws
exposes the lies disassembles the structure
and ravages the very foundation of evil.

Speak the truth to the people
To identify the enemy is to free the mind
Free the mind of the people
Speak to the mind of the people
Speak Truth.

Who Can Be Born Black

Who
can be born black
and not
sing
the wonder of it
the joy
the
challenge

Who
can be born
black
and not exult!

.... I

am a black woman
tall as a cypress
strong
beyond all definition still
defying place
and time
and circumstance
    assailed
        impervious
            indestructible

Look
    on me and be
renewed